IN THE MARGIN

A. C. CLARKE

INDEPENDENT INNOVATIVE INTERNATIONAL

Published by Cinnamon Press
Meirion House
Tanygrisiau
Blaenau Ffestiniog
Gwynedd, LL41 3SU
www.cinnamonpress.com
The right of A.C.Clarke to be identified as author of this work has been asserted by her in accordance with the Copyright, Designs and Patent Act, 1988. Copyright © 2015 A.C.Clarke
ISBN: 978-1-909077-95-9
British Library Cataloguing in Publication Data. A CIP record for this book can be obtained from the British Library.

Designed and typeset in Palatino by Cinnamon Press. Printed in Poland
Original cover design by Adam Craig.
Cinnamon Press is represented in the UK by Inpress Ltd www.inpressbooks.co.uk and in Wales by the Welsh Books Council www.cllc.org.uk

Acknowledgements

This book would not have come into being without the help and support of Jan Fortune of Cinnamon Press, whose patient and insightful mentoring has helped me to bring the poems into sharper focus and whose faith in the project has been a constant source of encouragement. Many poems have benefited also from the critical acumen of my dedicatees, the Caledonian Poets, and I am deeply indebted to many more, not least my earlier mentors Martyn Crucefix and Mario Petrucci, to John Glenday's Poetry Surgeries, to St Mungo's Mirrorball and to the Federation of Writers (Scotland). The weaknesses in the poems are all my own.

Versions of some of these poems have appeared in the following magazines and publications: *Artemis*, *The Cannon's Mouth*, Excel for Charity web-site, *Fras*, *Glasgow Review*, *Gutter*, *New Writing Scotland*, *New Voices Press* anthologies, *Orbis*, *Poetry News*, *Poetry Scotland*, *Segora anthology*, *PENning*, *Ver Poets anthologies*, *Weyfarers*, and on Troubadour, McLellan and Ilkley Poetry Competition web-sites.

'Woman Made of Glass' won the 2011 Grey Hen Competition. 'In Transit' won the 2012 Second Light Long Poem Competition. 'Aftermath' was runner-up in the 2012 Freda Downie competition. The first line of the poem is from a poem of Freda Downie's. 'My Private Collection' was runner-up in the 2012 Tryangle competition. 'Pandemonium' was runner-up in the Segora 2013 Poetry Competition. 'Cackhanded Scribe' was long-listed for the 2014 National Poetry Competition. 'Al Khatoon' was commissioned for the Hidden East project in 2013.

Quotations from *The Book of Margery Kempe* are from the edition by Barry Windeatt, D.S. Brewer, Cambridge 2004.

Contents

My Private Collection

A Year in Transit

Mirror Image

*To my fellow Caledonian Poets
for their unfailing support
and benignly critical advice.*

Or if perchance we stay our minds on aught
It is some picture in the margin wrought.
William Drummond

My Private Collection

Aftermath

Her mother snipes from the easy chair
by the fire, their only heating.
A poor bargain this plain daughter
when the neighbours talk of grandchildren
though the girl cooks and cleans and sews
as she always did, with care.

She nursed her father into his last
forgetfulness, visits his grave
with flowers each week, writes Christmas cards
to surviving aunts. She has time
between housework and counting out pills
to remember the past.

Though her face in the glass does not show
a ghost of its freshness in youth -
which was all she could claim of beauty -
she knows where the letters are hidden
strangled with scarlet ribbon
under her yellowing trousseau.

Margery Kempe on Dress

Hir clokes also wer daggyd and leyd with divers colowrs betwen the daggys, that it schuld be the mor staryng to mennys sygth
The Book of Margery Kempe, ll.260-262

Clothes! My undoing in my pride of youth,
a scandal when I sported white
on Christ's orders. How much I loved

the slub of wool thick-woven, the slink of silk,
brocades stiff with gilt. *Look at me*
cried the slashes in my cloak, its lining

peeping through like the scarlet mouth
of a wound. I braided my hair with gold,
outdressed my neighbours. I was a mayor's daughter.

You'd know me by my garments
any time. I could price cloth blindfold,
between finger and thumb, reckon

a woman's worth in a glance.
Christ said white, not cheap.
All eyes turned on me when I walked

in my transfigured raiment: it cost.
Tongues scourge me still for my virgin garb
draping a womb twice seven times childed.

Mary's colour becomes me.
Chosen for me.
I hold my head high.

Margery Kempe on Food

hyr confessowr was dyplesyd for sche ete no flesch, and so was mech of all
the company ... And therfor schamfully thei reprevyd hir
The Book of Margery Kempe, ll.1974-1976

No meat for me. I turned my lips
from spitroast, pastie, bone-broth.
Christ's flesh alone might enter a mouth

so given to his praise, houselled weekly
by gift of his grace. How often men,
women too, spat venom at me

grudging my fast, while they greased fingers
on pullet-wings, gobbets of pork.
Hypocrite they cried, who gave you the right

to spurn God-given food, pretend
to piety on a diet of worts?
We'll bring your high stomach down!

I was burned at the stake of their hatred.
Christ loves me the more. I know,
earth-penance done, I'll leap to his arms

fired by sacred hunger. Let them rail,
the nay-sayers. I have his word.

Ode to Tinned Salmon

You made your entrance
at family gatherings
a solid round
straight from the tin
grey film toning down
your lurid pink
or forked into chunks
either way
flanked by pale slices
of cucumber
on which Heinz salad cream
was poured
like a libation.

Doused in vinegar
to ward off germs
your tart flesh harboured
spinal bones
like necklaces of tiny
cotton reels.
Soft enough to crunch
for calcium
they wouldn't stick
in the craw.
You were the only fish I'd eat
without sifting each flake.

Highdays and holidays
you came into your own.
We tasted in you
luxury of food off ration
freedom of seas
no longer gunshipped
the glamour
of the dollared
unconquered West.

A Short History of Cooking

A forest fire roasted the first haunch.
Someone put two and two together

and those who huddled round the hearth
at the first ceremonial feast

breathed in the fumes of a thousand chippies
in that prophetic smoke.

Now their descendants stick plastic forks
into Big Macs, French fries,

watch the greasy wrappers skitter
in a December monsoon wind,

turn up the heat
in the world's oven.

Old Woman Cooking Eggs

from a painting by Velasquez

She draws your eyes across the gallery.
So different from half-naked goddesses
spilling plump flesh among tame greenery,
romantic landscapes, all waterfalls, crevasses,
tumbling cloud; from the tidy
hausfraus in chequered parlours, though she expresses
the fascination with the everyday
you find in such paintings. It's the way

she lives. Life leaps in the veins
that gnarl her knowing hands. She's still strong.
You can see it in her mouth, in the lines
of her cheek. Skilful. Eggs are simmering
in hot oil under her fingers. Signs
are, she's blind. She isn't looking
at the skillet, seems to be feeling for it, her spoon
hovering over the rim. Soon

she'll crack another egg and you know
it will slide in like the other two
whose whites fan out around unbroken yellow.
This is her kitchen. The good, sharp knife, the blue
and white jug, brass pestle and mortar go
with her serviceable gown. It's true
the young lad helping her looks sullen
as if he'd rather be off, but she'd discipline

any rebellion with a single glance
of her sightless eyes. And perhaps his frown
is one of concentration. He hasn't her acquaintance
with stoves and spitting fat. She's grown
old in service. Could be his granny. Once,
no doubt, she was kitchen-maid, wore her own frown.
Now she compels attention. You can't pass by.
Must watch her not watching eggs fry.

Haddock and Chips

We're sitting on the wall that edges a slipway
somewhere on South Tyneside. You've bought us

fish suppers after the long drive north,
the first meal of our new life.

I find the batter greasy: to say so
would strike the note you're waiting for.

It's late. The Tyne's a black strip flecked
with random lights: the road we'll take

out to your house will look like this
with fewer lights, under a sky

piling with clouds whose rust-red glare
gives back the city's distant neon.

The air's a damp muffler that clings
to nose and mouth. I should be hungry.

You watch me picking at white flakes of haddock
as if it were full of bones.

Welcome to Tyneside you say,
your voice a knife.

Midwife to Mother Shipton

Two days into her pains when she sent.
They warned me I'd turn flint-hearted:
her husband's seed, they said, made gravel in her,
troll-children cooled in her womb,
grey-faced, granite-skinned. Her money rang true

and I'm here in my blood and skin,
my heart beats sound as ever.
She too was warm and breathing,
cried in her pangs as any woman does. To the last
my fear was she or the child would be lost.

What pushed out of her tunnel of darkness
was nothing I could name: round as a boulder
sticky with blood, snagged with excrescences
a seethe of flesh, hair, bone
in which a spine unstrung its beads,

a tooth glinted. I told her a stillbirth.
Her fifth she said. I didn't show her
but wrapped it in the shawl she'd knitted,
tied the bundle as I might for kittens,
gave it to the river. It sank like a stone.

The Five Children of Mother Shipton

Rose quartz, firstborn, pink glitter under her skin,
already chilled to her crystal bones
though nothing to stop her living, far as we knew.
Her stillness drew the eye like a sculpture.
I never saw a lovelier child.

Tourmaline, a breech birth, skinny-ribbed,
swollen at wrist and ankle like a dropsical old man,
not a tinge of red from crown to clenched toes.
His blood lay torpid as a scummed pond.
He had a look of his father.

Jet wore his own mourning,
his spine a string of blackened beads
wrists amber bracelets.
His eyes rolled back, a white startle
in that withered peat-dark body.

Amethyst, blue-violet, a flaw in her heart.
We knew she wouldn't live
in our thick air, her pale eyelids
fluttered and fell, her lips
bruised dark as nightshade.

Toadstone, a botch, an unlicked mass,
a birthed tumour
the wrongness of the world made visible.
The river took that queasy bolus
at a single gulp.

Homunculus

Every day I check him, the little man I've brewed
from root, semen, dung.
Hunched in his flask
he looks at me out of a minikin face
 — heavy-lidded, frog-mouth on the grin —
my image and likeness. I watch him grow,
his budding limbs awaken, kick the glass,
his lips open, shut like a goldfish.
I can't hear him.

A mandrake shriek rips from his throat
the day I crack the crystal shell.
Out he hops, no bigger than my thumb,
perfect from pate to prick.
I coddle him in lambswool,
grub soil for worms, cull lavender for seeds,
fatten him tame. Daily
I stroke his rounding belly —
smooth as an egg - teach him to speak.

He calls to me now as he scuttles
among alembics, his squeal
drowned almost by the furnace roar.
I love to watch him. Though my schemes for gold
miscarry, he redeems all labours.
Forty days a-making
he never lay in woman's menstrue
to have his blood turned milk,
my imp, my devil's apple, my true son.

Sicilian Fairy

A shilling bought you tottering across the stage
on your thin legs; for a few more
you could be fed a biscuit, picked up, stroked.
You'd answer questions, your voice reed-thin
as the wind keening from a fairy mound.

Alive and dead you were rich pickings,
marked down for scalpels even as you were paraded
tricked out in doll-size finery for a bloated king,
your head no bigger than a baby's, your bones
too young for your age. Did you enjoy
your few weeks of fame, the crowds of gawpers?

You liked dressing up, wrote the doctor
who gave you to the dissectors, listing
among your symptoms sharp sight, love of glitter,
noted that you were *quick to recognise*
any person who had treated it kindly.

Wild Girl of Champagne

Some say she was a shipwrecked slave,
some, a squaw's daughter.
Under dead leaves the bones of her story
wait to be unearthed like children lost
in a fairytale wood far from home.

Thirst lured her from the trees: snared,
she tore the trussed fowl in the kitchen,
sprang the hide off a rabbit. In the field
she'd outrun hares, was keener in the chase
than any dog, dived duck-fashion in rivers.
Frogs were her dainty. She swallowed them
like bon-bons. Tipped a hopping armful
onto the plates of feasters once.

They christened her Marie. She learned good French.
She'd pass in time for native, every detail
- neat hair, gloved hands, shoes that couldn't run.
Only her eyes said different.

With their Mother's Milk

One version of the story of the 'wolf girls' Kamala and Amala

They woke latched to the dug,
nested against a grey mother
in a squirm of blindlings,
a smoor of milk, blood, dung,

her nourishment their comfort
until they licked her lips for meat
months on from when they should.
That was when the blood-thirst began.

They never sprouted fur but their nails
hooked, their teeth turned wolf.
After a time, fluent in yelp and howl,
they learned not to cry.

The sun burned them to a single colour,
the pads of their palms, knees, thickened.
Their jaws could crack bone.
Then the two-legs came

forced them into daylight, covered
their sex. They fought back,
happiest when the moon glowed blue
in eyes which shredded darkness

and they could sing to her
in their true voices,
throats slippery with flesh.
Their mouths would not easily learn

to relish cooking,
nor take to the words
crammed into them
to sweeten their tongues.

Inchkeith Experiment

How must it have been, learning the island
the huge sky, so often barred with steel,
its hanging lights too high to touch?
They could not say 'the grass is like...', 'the sea is like ...'
or grasp the messages waves smuggled in,
the shores of Fife remote as El Dorado.

They lived in each other's presence,
their days a blur of sight, smell, taste.
Perhaps, like looking into a silvered mirror,
they saw each other clear, the world they lived in
framed by absence. Perhaps, like looking into rippled water
they saw a hint of likeness forever

failing to resolve. Though they heard nothing
from the woman who tended them, her throat
locked since birth, they heard from gulls,
whose klaxon swooped out of the air;
patrolling oystercatchers swore at them;
sheep called their lambs to order: an island babel.

As, puppyish, they chased each other,
surely they made some noise?
Their tongues were not prisoned.
Did they wake one day
to find their mouths full of words?

Louise Bourgeois Woman

Look at her brass neck
the way her hair pulls back
from her figurehead brow

She thrusts desire in your gallery face
as you peer through your glasses
at a mist of curator's spiel

You guess if you touched her
how cold and hard she'd feel   how right
as if all along you'd known her contours

She's mistress of change
hangs double-sexed from a meathook
spools from her spider centre a dizzying thread

It's not the sudden shifts that make you queasy
it's how she reaches in scoops out your innards
holds out a hand that doubles as a fist

My Private Collection

smells of stuffed birds moulting, mothballs, ether.
I walk the shiny linoleum between cases
where dogfish hang suspended like lifeboats,
enter one room through an aisle of whale-ribs,
a room of narwhal skulls, each rapiered jaw
fineboned as the unicorn's brow.

Trays of pierced butterflies spread wings whose sheen
dulled long ago, here are corals and sponges
brittling in the parched air, colour leached,
sets of teeth on the grin, knucklebones, ox-horns.
Tucked in a drawer wadded with packing, eggs
which never will hatch. A second drawer

holds beetles ranged by size, glazed over time
to monochrome. I am searching for something -
not this timber wolf's faked snarl, canines gleaming,
against a painted backdrop; nor that tattered bear
propped on hindlegs, claws impotently curved.
The exit, perhaps? It is arrowed in neon green

but darkness is falling. Through tall windows
I see trees flail their branches, earth nurse its wounds
under a tarmac bandage. Christmas lights
swing wildly, roped from gibbet to iron gibbet.
In here the temperature never varies,
nothing moves except in slow

degeneration. I am at home with that stasis,
the hush that coats the rooms thick as ash.
If I stepped outside I might hear on the wind
the voices of rain which are the voices of children.
I might remember what I put aside
like clagged boots at the door.

Enlightened

I hope you'll clean the bench where you put your mucky boot

Out of the blue-grey morning
which has just got out of bed
and touches everything with the same spare light -
ice-puddle, narrow bus-station bench,
sour lips of this woman —
I am jerked back to my child-self,
those women who knew I did things wrong.

My boot isn't muddy. The bench I wipe
under her stare, hasn't a speck of dirt.
I tell her I'm sorry. She's not having any,
perches her narrow backside
on a ledge not meant for sitting,
stares. In her pinched-up face I see
years of mistrust,
of having to fight her way, every step.

When the bus comes, I stand behind her.
She's scrabbling for change,
joshing the driver; *smiling*.
I watch the winter fields roll past
their intricate, unnamable colours
brightening with the brightening sun.

Cleg

A sharp jab like a phlebotomist's needle,
blood drawn
      cloud like a bodybag of thin material
      folds round me. Through grey haze
      a glimpse of toy-size farm, a sunlit valley.

A throb like a tourniquet being tightened
round my upper arm
      at the top of the hill
      in cloud or sun the lochan cups black water,
      sheep and late lambs search for the sweeter grass.

An itch that won't be scratched to silence,
skin losing its cool
      on the home stretch
      sun bounces off tarmac; meadowsweet,
      vanilla-sickly, clouds the ditches.

Red swelling, angry as a sunset, the body
turning on itself
      outside the window
      clouds pile-drive long shafts of water
      into baked earth, thunder revs its engine.

An areole of blisters circles
a puncture mark that's hard to see
but will prove slow to heal
      after the rain
      clouds ride in acres of uneasy blue
      unshaded gardens stoke, like furnaces,
      blinds are drawn.

The pharmacist
has remedies for everything, almost.

Fingers Crossed

Spilt salt reddens in a pool of wine.
You heap it with the flat of your knife.

Yesterday a mirror cracked: its jagged faultline
split my face. I read how someone found

a Celtic head in a junkshop, cradled it home,
set it on her bedside table for luck.

The creature that it harboured woke,
loped down stairs in its wolf-pelt. The house shivered.

I think of a skinned rabbit, pink as a baby,
laid at the foot of a standing stone; remember

the mess of bone and feather in the cellar.
Something cries in the dark outside.

All the lights are on. The fridge is humming.
I tell myself everything will be fine.

Pompeiians

The day the sky caved in and all they'd known
turned ash – gods helpless in their shrines,
hearth-spirits scuttling for boltholes –

words were already beginning to rumble,
spill over their heat-shocked skin

and ever since have rained like lapilli
burying them deeper. Even the shapes
their bodies left define an absence.

We will never know these citizens
who gaze out of mosaics, turn a bronze smile

to a lost garden, fondle a painted lover.
Though we catch an echo of laughter or anger
from a dead tongue, the voice we strain to hear

dwindles to the rattle of a sistrum,
wind-chimes shivered by the ghost of a breath.

Casualty

Who are you, bundled on the sidewalk
like household rubbish?

I am nothing
debris of an ordinary day

What were you,
under this sun which does not forgive,
under this sky which does not weep?

I was a strong hand waving
a mother's kiss
a child's running feet

Why did you stay here in the killing city
after the soldiers came?

My home is here
my father's father's home.
I speak with the city's voice

How shall I mourn you
how remember you?

Do not shed tears.
Their bitter salt
rusts all bright hopes

Do not sing funeral hymns
their cadences fall heavy

Do not bring flowers
their petals spill

Give me a shape,
a human shape again
build me in words
name me

Memorial

Remember them - those years of sweat and drink,
of money - hard-muscled men who took risk light
as ropewalkers, downed their drams at the Tight Line
after hours at the rockface, arms blue-penned
with twining anchors, dragons, hearts,
hands skinned by broken stone. Hundreds
came off with little worse. The way luck goes.

Remember them. Like offerings thrown
to a water-god their broken bones
pay for the wounded mountain. They join
unnumbered comrades: centuries of graft
buried where spoilheaps toppled, a tunnel caved
or missed footing brought a steeplejack down.
Pause as you flick a switch. Count fifteen.

Silence

Remembrance Day Nov 11

They do it for us
those bareheaded leaders
in greatcoats,
fixed in black and white
since the eleventh hour
in front of the great white
sham as they wait for the drumroll
of heavy artillery, the scream
of flypast.

They believe themselves
as those did who shot lads
at dawn, wrote letters
I regret to say your son…
perform prescribed rites
to sanctify
desert patrols, the tedium
of death-in-waiting
the two minute frenzy
that leaves a child in ruins.

They do it for us
so that we need not hear
the question in a poppy
white as a corpse
the confused cries
of those set free to die
the old lie, the old lie.

They do it for us
sporting their poppies
like novice hunters blooded.
Nothing is said. Not here.
Not in the villages
whose obelisks, obscure with names,
carry their complement of sodden wreaths.
Not in libraries, schools, prisons.

Break this silence,
break ranks.

The Poem

The poem is my motherland, my refuge, my friend and my travelling companion
Adnan Al-Sayegh

I carried a poem in my pocket as cash
for those who won't take plastic,
carried it across grey level plains,
each more featureless than the last
into crowded cities, each more like the next
until I settled - the way a butterfly
settles - in a place
foreign as its people's moonfaces,
their blurred vowels.

And the poem
turned itself into a room:
I was inside its words
safe as houses.

Then tanks came, helicopter gunships
police who said
we are only protecting you
who said
don't say we didn't warn you

 soldiers who huffed and puffed
and blew the poem inside out
so I stood homeless
in the ruined street,
words strewn on the sidewalk
running black in gutters.
I heard their groans.

I took a taxi to the airport
to catch the last plane to somewhere else.
My eyes stung with salt
as I searched the aisle for a seat.
When I slid in beside her,
a woman turned and smiled:

Don't fret, the poem said,
I'm coming with you.'

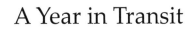

A Year in Transit

A Year in Transit

5 September IRA terrorists bomb the Park Lane Hilton hotel killing 2 and injuring 63

i

What if I could go back
to that long-shut seaside Mecca

with the redplush fleapit seats
foxed mirrors in the ladies

see as I twirled in crippling stilettos,
my cheap dress sequined by revolving light,

the months stretch out like tarmac
towards their end? What if I turned

from my luck, returned to the kitchen,
the listed tasks, the soaked cloths drying ?

October 9 a bomb explosion outside the Green Park tube station
near Picadilly in London kills 1 and injures 20

ii

When I think of you I think of the sea,
which you loved, grey battleships

logged in *Jane's Fighting Ships* with meticulous
zeal, an evening in the *Still and West*

watching the flow of traffic downriver,
your eyes that milky blue we see

in pebbles, your gaze remote.
In my one photo you look like a yachtsman,

the ocean-going sort, impatient to turn
to the harbour, your folded arms

defending the heart under your seaman's sweater.
Who are you smiling for?

iii

That Christmas Eve we hear gunshots
think them a motorbike backfiring

until we turn on the news. To me
a bomb factory in my former street

feels exciting. Hardly real.
But you don't seem real either

out of the north with your golden beard
and freedom. I can't fathom

why violence at two removes
should put you in a rage.

iv

Good days, transparent blue's tossed back
from water to salt air, heatless and clear

as if the thinnest glass is all
that keeps the island from escaping

and we might chime infinity against it,
or shattering a flaw swoop up

into forever. Today the sky is thick
and grey as lisle, a stocking-mask,

the roads run muted, which in sunny hours
lift, sing towards the chalk dazzle rimming

the coast. We are the only visitors
to a museum I never knew existed

until you brought us. Light crawls in and dies
beside arrangements of stuffed mice

in bridal gowns, birds strumming guitars
with grounded wings, and without explanation,

at start or end — depending on your route —
a single, severed hand, palm outwards.

December 29 a bomb explosion at La Guardia Airport kills 11

V

Giggling like schoolkids, we choose
the tiger's eye for my ring finger,

I've no idea it's my birthstone. Changeling,
its tawny sheen safe silicate —

the true child lethal blue — its yellow slit
narrows or widens as light falls.

I catch its sideways glance, as I turn
the silver setting, savour the weight and fit,

splay my hand under the strip-light
as if it were hitched to the future.

20 January Emily Jackson is stabbed to death in Leeds

vi

They're testing sound levels in the bar
which has seen better days, and a woman

not pretty, not young, opens her voice
to sing *Paper Roses* for just us two.

She sings with conviction.
You'd sent me flowers for Valentine's —

I think it was you. The song swells over the speakers
drowns our talk. Just now I'd give a bunch

to be that woman proudly delivering
imitation love without missing a beat.

vii

On the chalk cliffs, rain driving against us,
we're kissing hard, can't tell

if the salt on our tongues is our own taste or air
nor if the water running down our cheeks

is flung by wind or whipped from our eyes.
Our hair tangled together, we cling to each other

as if we could tent ourselves from weather.
I want it never to end. Down in the bay

a grey hump-backed sea paws at the stack
arched like the nave of a ruined cathedral.

When we dry off in the pub with its smoking fire
your eyes rove over panelling, fake

horse brasses, looking for something. The bar
is empty. In an hour we'll drive away

rain sheeting across your line of vision
soon as the wipers clear the screen,

the cliffs behind us in their old routine:
slow attrition, random, shattering fall.

viii

Half a mile in, gibbons drop to the car-roof,
bounce and chatter, charming the children,

who don't see the scratches, wouldn't care
if they did. You frown because I laugh.

We wander the topiary garden
pointing out white peacocks, in a vague

Sunday afternoon malaise. Under distant elms
couched lions chew their paws or noisily yawn.

We will exhaust the possibilities
sooner than expected. You stop off

on the way home, in a field where souped-up bangers,
all rattle and sputter, tear round a dirt track

revving like angry bees, the summer air
hazed with fumes, sweet stink of leaked fuel.

ix

We take the path, as thousands have,
pretend we're family. Along the Nidd

trees dip their weight of leaves, the turf,
under today's rare sun, unfolds

plump, glistening curves. Paired swans
tow their complement of cygnets.

If we say nothing, the spell might hold.
But here's the cave, its stalled cascade

like elflocks, iron-grey streaked yellow,
draping a bony shoulder: underneath,

strung where they catch the drips, a jumble
of cast-offs — kettles, besoms, toys —

wait to be hardened, layer on layer,
until they merge to outcrop. Look!

A teddybear hangs by the neck,
a child's love, furring to stone.

21 July   Christopher Ewart-Biggs, UK ambassador to Ireland,
and a civil servant, Judith Cooke, are killed by a landmine at
Sandyford, Co. Dublin

X

Scotch Corner, where the south
admits its end, the point of no return

for me, even now. I never see the sign
without a tremor. How many hours we spent

in transit, happiest aiming for
the skyline, miles of tarmac

spewed behind us. I have no names
for streets we drove through, sullen terraces

one after other on the Wearside roads,
one town drab as the next. Sometimes

at dusk we'd be on a back road, black hedges
blocking the view each side, when without warning

a lighted driveway swept into sight
a gabled building, every pane ablaze

for the guests you pledged we'd join one day
at *the best hotel in the north* or some such.

And once, passing the high stone gate
of a manorial park, I swear

white cattle glimmered through the darkening trees
as if your words had willed them there.

4 September - Peace March in Derry attracts 25,000 people in a
call to end violence in Northern Ireland

xi

Comes back to me the stone cottage, its door
open on sooty walls — do I imagine

those? — the reek of peat and oak,
a blackboard chalked with news of the catch,

amber kippers flattened from the spine
into the ace of spades, or hearts

their sea-smoke tang new to my taste,
buttery juices running down my chin

as I winkle hairfine bones from my teeth,
swallow your story hook, line, sinker.

15 October –

Two members of the Ulster Defence Regiment jailed for 35 years for murder of the members of the Republic of Ireland cabaret performers Miami Showband.

xii

Will you remember these woods? All our times
that count are outdoors, where

we don't take up space — too much of us
in a borrowed bed. We can breathe.

The air doesn't mind us nor the trees
yearning upwards, the lichened stones.

The dry-twig mesh printing my back
unreadably signals we're here

on sufferance, all the same. Commotion
in the leaves above, sharp exchange,

silence. The sky is white light through
spruce-green lattice I could watch for hours.

When we leave, our steps are gunshots
scattering wings. You shove the car

in gear for the last hill. We won't be back.
It's chilly now. Ahead the road winds down

past chequered sunlight to the levels
where townships smudge the coast. Already

their haze works in, fogging our throats.
If we kissed, we would tongue sulphur, dust.

10 December 1976 Betty Williams and Mairead Corrigan awarded the Nobel Peace Prize for their work in promoting peace in Northern Ireland

Mirror Image

Magdalene

She's folded more than sixty years
into the linen cupboards. When she started
they had the smoothing irons — you heated them up
on the kitchen range, made sure you wrapped a cloth
round your fingers to lift them — and grey soap
that'd scour your skin like pumice, the penitents' hands
red raw with it. She was fit to drop
that first day, but she couldn't sleep

for the baby crying. They'd taken hers
already. This one mewled for hours.
You'd want to comfort the wee soul. She asked
next morning but the nuns said she'd dreamt it;
the girls couldn't answer — if they spoke
they'd get the rough end of a tongue or a belt.
She said a prayer, knew it wouldn't work.
Next night was quiet but she lay awake

with the pain in her breasts where they'd bound them flat
 — still full of milk. Days and nights merged
into one long cycle. Girls left or disappeared.
She stayed on. When the convent shut
they'd washing machines, and irons with thermostats,
no more starch. She's on the same estate
as some of the Sisters – odd to think of that.
They don't speak. But what

gives her the shivers, she saw on telly
the other night, they'd dug the convent grounds
ready for building, turned up bones
                — girls gone missing, babies.
Sure, they wouldn't! No - they'd have given her own
to the Christian Brothers, he'll be a big man now.
Perhaps she's passed him in the street, not known.
She'd ask, but all the ones who'd know are gone.

John and Margery Debate her Dress Style

And when hir husbond wold speke to hir to levyn hir pride sche
answeryd schrewedly and schortly and seyd that sche was comyn of
worthy kenred – hym semyd never for to a weddyd hir.
The Book of Margery Kempe, ll.263-265

Always one for airs and graces, you,
dress like an alderman's wife when I'm plain John Kempe.
Leave off!

Alderman! My father was <u>mayor.</u>
You married above your station. It behoves
I dress to my rank. My money pays.

While it lasts. Why not live like others?
Want, want, want – that's you!
People talk. Why fall out with the neighbours?

They're eaten up with envy, sourfaces all.
It tickles my heart to hear them gripe.
The more they whine the richer my garb.

Pride's no less a deadly sin. Come, Margery,
be reasonable, cut your coat
according to my cloth. Learn contentment.

Your cloth's a threadbare weave that's shrunk
to miser's fit. Contentment's a name
sluggish souls give to sloth.

You'll always have the last word, if you can.
Ay John, that's one thing we agree on.

Margery Kempe on Brewing

I took up brewing in my worldly days,
three or four years the talk of the place
for ale, though new to the trade.

Then all went flat. Try what I would,
brew after brew raised a fine head
only to fall. I lost much goods.

Not content, I must needs turn miller,
hired a good man, strong team for the wheel.
Not long before they jibbed, stock still

spite of whip and spur. None after
would work for me, men called me cursed.
In all this I see God's mercy,

I do! I could have made a mint
but He had other ideas. He'd make me a saint.

To a Train Ticket

Orange and cream *vade mecum*
no bigger than a Garibaldi biscuit
mere card
not even the dignity
of plastic
you open doors to a future
miles from the present.

Pointless like all forgotten currencies
when your time's up
until then potent
as a signature
on a letter of conduct.

I delve for your three-inch reassurance
in the depths of a bag
proffer you
to be clipped or scrawled
five hundred miles
pinched
between finger and thumb.

The Only Woman in the Painting

leans her head on her left hand. Her right
appears to hold a cigarette. Perhaps
she's going to stub it out. Her eyes are narrowed.
Her expression says *I've heard this before*
says *Business is bad tonight*, says
I hope it's not the one with the green shirt.

She's resting one scarlet leg
(matching tights, shoe) on a stool and she's leaned
so far forward her right breast is saved
from nakedness only by the cup
of her black bustier. The pubbing poets
look at each other, or the middle distance.

Was she put in to indicate Bohemia?
Is she some sort of Muse?
Or is it that her leg's diagonal
crosses neatly behind Macaig's grey trousers,
her tights pick up
the colour of MacDiarmid's scarf?

Crab Supper

There's fishing boats still at the staithe
where fishwives used to cry the herring

gleaming in crateloads, red-rimmed eyes
a mute reproach. It's winter dusk,

a blood-red sun dropping behind
the far bank of the Tyne, blank windows

fill with light, an hour's last grace,
goldleaf illumines the scrawled river.

The cobbles reek as you bring me down
to the end of the quay, where a pailful of crabs

jostle each other. We bag a couple,
drive home swerving round blind corners,

cats eyes gleam, go out. You promise a treat,
in your wife's kitchen take a hammer,

split the shells clean down the middle
scoop out the flesh. You know what you're doing.

I taste the white meat, its faint salt
the dark meat, dangerously rich.

Al-Khatoon

You are the soul of the land,
Men can see you if they would
in the shiver of snow on a mountain
the moon in her mist-drapes
a bee-eater's
green lightning.

Your bones stiffen mountains, your blood
courses in fertile rivers.
Here in these gaunt high plateaux
you are most visible
most feared
but there's no corner of the world
the iciest waste
the thirstiest desert
your breath does not sweeten.

The pangs of your labour
split the earth
your groans raise waves like towers
you weep fire
Al-Khatoon,
black as Kali
who was born out of stone

yet how tender the fingers
which stroke awake first shoots of wheat
how gentle the song
with which you lull the long day
asleep. Not one of your nurslings
uncherished
even when you rage.

...

You will not see life squandered
for a narrow text
bodies you fashioned so exactly
slit for a whim
by hands you fashioned.
You will take all back
to your dark bosom
in your own time
men women children
all faiths and none
all the bruised bodies, minds.
They will call it death ...

smiling, you will open your hands
let the stars fly out like doves.

Cackhanded Scribe

In the scriptorium, stooped over vellum,
others ink in blue sprigs of vein,
outline muscles in carmine, finesse
the contours of a mandible, no need
to knife out errors, they know the pattern backwards,
never, distracted by a sneeze, a fly,
miss out toe or finger, add one too many.

He, in his carrel, practising
in a side aisle still, after all these years,
scratches across the page, sheds gouts of ink,
sketches a monopod under its monstrous
foot-shade, a rhino-hide monoceros,
bat-eared demon, confounds rumour and truth
in one-eyed babies, hydatidiform jumbles,

outfreaking choirstall ruderies: marginalia.
They never let him loose on the main,
the blueprint for Vitruvian Man,
but shelve each botched attempt delivered
alongside all the perfect manuscripts
like a bad Quarto which must be collated
against the good, to fix the definitive text.

Golem

The rabbis followed God, took mud,
slapped it to shape — not pretty,
they lacked the touch — but serviceable,
speechless too, a boon
in one who serves. To bring it to life
they wrote on the dull forehead.

A slow thing, heavy-limbed,
apt to shatter the least pot with a touch.
Faithful as a dog. Suddenly fierce.
Stronger than any wrestler. Its fury
bashed enemies to sludge; hard to call off
once roused, if crossed could turn,
bite the hand that made it. They say

one has been lying dormant in an attic
somewhere in Middle Europe for decades
though flesh and blood creatures
died by the million. What cataclysm
could summon from brute sleep
the vengeance it's dreaming,
write it true again?

Leonardo's Travel List

spectacles, bone-saw, sheets of paper
listed in the same widdershins script
as the notes spidering round the womb he draws
lifted into daylight, split like a conker
to show the child which, crouching, seems
to hide its eyes against exposure.

He's need of spectacles to scan
fine detail down to the five perfect toes
on each crossed foot, a steady hand
to carry out this strange Caesarean.
Do his lenses mist over? If so,
no doubt he wipes them briskly, works on,

focused on what the probing blade will show.
He's come a fair distance for this.
The mirror-writing (*inkhorn, pens*)
tumbles his thoughts across the folio
as if they've spilled from the right hemisphere
unchecked. That all-consuming need to know

drives him to go in deep, get visceral,
cut to the truth behind the fluent drapes
of donnas and madonnas. She'll be no saint,
the woman he splits open (*forceps, scalpel*).
He'll wash his hands of her when he's done,
change clothes, spruce up (*stockings, comb, shirt, towel*).

Wild Peter

i

His name was given him, as a new name
is given to a bought dog, engraved

on the collar they made him wear
after he went missing. He learned it
as a dog learns to come to the master's call.

His name was one of two things he could say.
The other was 'King George'.

ii

He was wild because he was found in a forest
He was wild because he made a humming noise
He was wild because he had shocking table manners

He was wild because he would not sleep in a bed
He was wild because he was good at climbing trees
He was wild because his nails needed clipping

He was wild because he kept his hat on
He was wild because he liked sucking twigs
He was wild because he was charmed by a watch

He was wild because he would dance to the fiddle
He was wild because he did not powder his hair
He was wild because he mourned his master like a
dog.

iii

And they painted his portrait
And they raised his headstone
And his grave is still visited by flowers.

Mirror Image

i

When I was a wolf, before words,
life was hunger, fullness, hunting, sleep.
What I did not understand I ran from.

Came the day when, having outrun the pack,
I stopped to drink at a forest pool,
dipped my tongue. A new creature

stared up at me out of a sick face,
tongue busy. I did not stay
to see if it could breach the water.

Once I looked back: the glades
were full of their mysterious light,
the world in its usual order.

Nothing dogged me but my own shadow.
That night in our den I sat apart,
the moon was up, our hunting mother,

and everyone began to sing.
My voice caught in my throat, like a furball.

ii

A figure walks towards me, naked,
skin tanned leather, breasts a parenthesis
in a body hardwired for flight.

She drops to all fours, her spine
arches, her dugs hang loose, her muzzle lifts
in a snarl. I grin, show my residual fangs.

Her blue glare swivels towards me. Her jaws gape.
Out of that blood-dark cavern a cry
which does not break the glass but climbs

my own throat. A hunter's moon
behind her furred head, like a halo.

Traveller's Tale

On the horizon I saw white gazelles
in a single unbroken stream, like milk from a pitcher.
Loping beside them, the boy,

lithe brown animal, his mane
lifted by the wind of his speed. For days
I stalked him, tried to pin him down.

He lapped from pools, rooted up wild radish,
alert in every muscle. Sometimes
he'd stand upright, search rock crevices

for lizards. His teeth were flat as a cow's,
the sounds he made (though seldom) all gazelle.
I brought the tale back but no photograph,

made a second journey, tried to net him
in all his naked wonder. He startled
at the chopper's drone as it hovered over.

Was never going to be more than my word.

Maeve's Bull

Thanks to Alexander Hutchison who gave me this story and the phrase about Maeve's thighs

Maeve and her husband, the king with the unpronounceable
name,
set to: a flyting, not of words but of worldly goods.
First his retainers, three hundred stout kerns
in leather cuirasses, oak staves in their fists,
lined up against the length of the Great Hall of Connaught
six deep. She matched him man for man.

Next, on the cleared and fresh-swept flagstones, gold.
He opened every ironbound chest, every least purse,
tumbled the coinage of a dozen client kingdoms
in a dragon-bait of winking metal. The courtiers
covered their eyes. 'Match that!' She snapped her fingers.
Two treasuries weighed in the balance, carat for carat.

So it went on: his garnet-studded torc of the serpent finials,
her necklace, twisted silver from the mines of the east,
his bearskin cloak, her ermine collar, his helmet plumed
with the tailfeathers of ospreys, her swansdown tippet.
The four corners of the inhabited earth crammed
into fifty feet by twenty. The courtiers dropped to their knees.

When each had thrown into the contest every last ring,
brooch, bracelet, nose-stud, not a dress-pin's difference
between them
for value, they wrestled each other in wealth of the fields.
In all Ireland were never such swift horses, such plump flocks,
such milk-heavy cows. The courtiers fell on their faces:
sure this queen and king were made for each other!

Then Maeve of the hospitable thighs saw him:
a bull magnificent in muscle, white-horned
Finnbennach, the Father of all prize animals,
malehood in its pure, untampered strength.
And she had none like him. Queen though she was
she had none like him. Queen, though, she was,   ...

68

and not to be soon bested. It came to her ears
that the Daire of Cooley had such a bull
as pygmied her husband's: a hundred warriors
could sleep in the shade of his horns. He shafted
fifty heifers a day and each one calved.
'I'll have that bull!' she vowed and sent her servants

with gifts of gold, of silver, of cows for the loan of it,
gift of her thighs for the loan of it. 'Done!' cried the Daire.
Till the gossiping wind strolled by, told him her servants
boasted that had he refused, she'd have taken it anyway.
'Right!' cried the Daire, 'No bull!' Maeve had vowed to have it.
And what Maeve vowed to have, Maeve had.

Thousands of dead warriors later
the bull was hers for the taking where he lay
gasping his life out on the field of Cooley.
Thus did the flyting of Maeve and her king
end in blood. Thus the silver-tongued wordspinners
make a tale of a few brass rings and two starved cattle.

Pandemonium

We turn the corner, full into the stink
from his sweat-trap of curls, where he stands on the steps
surveying his flock. You gag.
He gives off undiluted male
from back-raked horn to cloven hoof. Sooty as hell
with a voice like a foghorn with quinsy, the cocksure stance
of *droit de seigneur,* no hiding him. Never.

He jigs through the psalters, merry devil
enlivening margins, leers from the backside of choir seats,
priapic, won't be bowdlerised; see his statue,
the antidote to talking heads, the goat-god
who in full view of marble sages drives
between the furry haunches of his woman,
frowning with lust. She'll be full of him come spring.

Underneath all, wild music: the raggedy man's
headlong rush through cow-parsley, oak-stand,
tootling his hornpipe to a discord of rooks;
hellebore's carrion stench trumpeting
bee-sweet nectar; the shout
of an arum spike; the come and get it
song of scent-glands under a she-goat's tail.

In Praise of Bogs

Praise to the beautiful treachery of bogs, oases
among the drabs of fescue and bentgrass, enlivened
by wisps of cottonsedge, yellow stars of that asphodel
which likes its roots bathed in continual peat-soup.

Look from a height into a sodden glen, you'll see
a burn snaking the length of the luminous flats
where sphagnum rolls out an illusive matting
between the armoured hills, begging you to come down,
walk on water. If you set out at night
across an unknown heath, take your wits with you.

Don't let the flickering hobby lanterns dance you
into a quag. Too many have been sunk.
From time to time
a spade strikes on a drowned and leathery skin
holding its shape as if the bones
had stepped out minutes ago, some iron age queen
acid-red hair flaring around the blackened
ruin of her beauty, some victim
drugged on sacred gruel, strangled
to keep the land sweet as bog-butter.

Move quick and light from tuft to tuft
of barely-anchored grass, not stopping an instant –
a bog may let you cross. Drop in a coin
for safe conduct. A bog will not forget.

Swarm

There in the afternoon sun
it sways a little,
hums. A few stragglers
dither outside, then settle.

Hidden under heaving pelts
the queen draws them, sure
as iron files to a magnet
deep in the core.

Let her escape they'll rise
a black and amber cloud,
striped ballerinas pirouetting air
their little daggers clenched
between honeyed thighs.

Leap

Earth, moon-crescent against endless black,
curves under his outstretched foot as he
launches into deep trust: science and luck
both. Ground comes rushing up in a hurry
of welcome. He somersaults in freefall,
straightens, pulls the ripcord on a glissando
through backlit air. Fields, highways, bridges all
the well-known man-marks lay themselves before him
in slow prostration. Time to breathe easy, yield
to earth's persistent tug, drift treewards, skim
the branches, saunter down: everything held.

In The Museum

Baked into this wall, imperial
guards look out aslant, each pupil
blank. Assyria's bit of rough.

Here is the hawkhead god
whose hissing spite can just be heard
if you lean close enough.

Rome in her marble regimentals
licensed to kill for Senate and People
(now fighter planes shell out democracy

where client kings obeyed)
the staples of an ancient trade
displayed as the high art of weaponry,

Trident's three-pronged spear
— at one touch cities disappear —
no less an ornament of Mars.

How should we not give reverence to war
edging ever nearer to super-nova?
In our blood runs the violence of stars.

Well

for IH

You came looking for rest
found a bed of nails.
You searched for an oasis:
they gave you
a fouled stairwell in a scheme highrise.

You have become a wanderer
who may never pitch tent
in the land of your fathers
nor ever call a place
truly home.

Here where rain slants across a window
blurring the future
where the loveliest landscape
cannot equal the heart's
insistent memory
one gleaming afternoon
you might still find
hidden under briars
half-choked with rubble
a well springing from the same
deep source
that made your childhood holy.

Stoop to it
gather in your palms
its trembling water
in which for a brief moment sun
steps out of the sky.

May that moment be
a strange, beautiful coin
you keep in your purse
simply to look at
and smile.

How the Cailleach Bheur created Loch Awe

She went to bed and left the stopper out,
letting the mountain gusher decant gallons
into the strath: homesteads, cattle, spelt
choked on the drink. Only higher ground
poked here and there through the brimming loch
that was yesterday's pasture. Hardly had she time
to rub the sleep out of her eyes and gape
before the gods of weather struck.

She crouches near the summit, petrified
into perpetual penitence. Few note her
as they clamber scree-slopes, bent on their Munro haul
though some glance back to where the water shines
silver with promise like a lucky coin
that falls so pat it seems no accident.

Woman Made of Glass

She can't remember a time
before she knew to be careful.
No-one told her. She *knew.*

Her mother used to squeeze her hand so tight
she felt it crack. She's never risked touch since,
spent childhood dodging

the heavy arms of aunts,
washing the smears
of fishmouth kisses from her skin.

She saw a glass frog once, its guts
clustered in its belly like pale grapes,
its small heart pittering:

took to covering herself –
high collars, sleeves to wrists,
thick tights. *Like an old maid*

said her mother. *No boyfriends yet?*
the aunts would dig. Afraid of heat
she'd hurry past lovers fused

mouth to mouth in doorways,
likes cool places still,
country churches on weekday afternoons,

the saints in the windows filtering light
through sightless eyes.
Old glass is her favourite: its pieced

stories jewel-bright, simple, remote
as fairy-tale. Does she notice
how sometimes it bulges towards the base

thick and opaque, as if all these years
it's been sneaking out of the leaden cames,
slipped down, let itself go?

Sister, I have a job for you

We have to cut out Mr Hardy's heart.
His surgeon's voice cuts into her free time.
Twenty-three, newly courting, she wants out —
her boy will be impatient. Hardy's name

means a cantankerous old man, that's all.
She has no choice but help him, though her training
has not been on cadavers. *Sister, scalpel.*
Scissors. Swab. He's looking now for something

to put the heart in. Gets a biscuit tin
out of the kitchen, clears the crumbs. *We're done.*
Off she bikes. She doesn't have an inkling
how the dead poet might have urged her on

feeling his tinned and towel-wrapped heart recover
its noon-tide throb if he had seen her go
speeding along the lanes to meet her lover
hair streaming like his Emma's long ago.

At the Reading

i

Words rise into the space above the desk
with its piles of trapped poems,
through the ceiling, the roof-void, the slates
on, on through the Karman line,
past the orbit of the moon, out beyond Pluto,
voyaging into silent Sargassos,
where wreckage of forgotten stars
drifts and tangles, spawning-grounds for worlds.

ii

Words raise in the space above the desk,
a garden, a child and his mother, rose-shadows
sliding across her face as she smiles at him.

A shadow shifts: casually the child
unzips himself throat to navel, displays for an instant
his heart where it cowers afraid of itself.
We look again. The child plays, the mother smiles,
the garden moves in and out of sunshine.

We saw it though. We saw the whole thing. And we see
how the desk and the books and the plastic seats
and the serviceable walls have gone a long way off,
like looking through the wrong end
of a telescope. And here are our minds
developing an image burned in by light.
Here in this room is the poet reading his words.
We could not say if he draws light to him
or filters light or is light itself.

Notes

Sicilian Fairy

Sicilian Fairy is the nickname of Caroline Crachami, a primordial dwarf exhibited in Georgian England, whose skeleton is now in the Hunterian Museum in London. The words in italics are from Sir Edward Home's *Lectures on Comparative Anatomy.*

Memorial

Fifteen men were killed during the construction of Cruachan power station.

How the Cailleach Bheur created Loch Awe

Cailleach Bheur: Old Hag of the Ridges.

Sister, I have a job for you

After his death Hardy's heart was removed for burial in the village he was born in; the rest of his body is interred in Westminster Abbey.